ANDREW MARTIN

INTERNATIONAL
INTERIOR DESIGN
REVIEW

VOLUME 6

MARTIN WALLER • DOMINIC BRADBURY

ANDREW MARTIN

INTERNATIONAL

EDITOR: MARTIN WALLER

TEXT: DOMINIC BRADBURY

PROJECT EXECUTIVE: ANNIKA BOWMAN

PRODUCT DESIGN: GRAPHICOM DESIGN

First Published in 2002 by

ANDREW MARTIN
INTERNATIONAL

ISBN 0-9530045-3-8

Reproduction by Yale Press. Printed in Great Britain by Butler and Tanner.

ACKNOWLEDGMENTS

The author and publisher wish to thank all the owners and designers of the projects
featured in this book.

They also thank the following photographers:

Richard Waite, Alaisdair Smith, Carla Antoni, Mike Hall, Craig Frazer, Brandon Coetzee, Stefan Antoni,
William Cummings, Pete Hopkins, Chicago Tribune photos by Bill Hogan, Yavuz Draman, Bob Allen,
Dries Van Den Brande, Winifried Heinz, Miguel Tres, Carlos Dominguez, David Montgommery, Marc Stanes,
Henry Bourne, Tim Beddows, Keith Collie, Nick Hufton/VIEW, Alex Sarginson, Simon Rix,
Mona Gundersen, Margareth de Lange, Gilles Trillard, Jeremy Young, Patrick Tyberghein, Hans Fonk,
Jan Verlinden, Pere Planells, Trevor at AC Cooper, Jose Lasheras, Mark Luscombe-Whyte,
Miti Info Image Monaco, Christine Gerondeau, Ray Main, Darren Chatz, Andreas von Einsiedel,
Jean-Marc Palisse, Roberto Battistini, Iain Kemp, Alberto Riginiq, Matthew Weinreb, Ugur Atag,
Michael Stepanov, Ulso Tsang, Joseph Sy, Ariadne Ahrens.

introduction

Interiors are supposed to be less prone to the fickle wind of fashion than the catwalks. Designers are expected to create classic schemes that will pass the test of time. The truth is less simple. We are all subject to the hothouse culture of the media. It is impossible not to be influenced by the passions of the moment. Indeed anyone who remains oblivious to them would disappoint the beholder in whose eye beauty certainly would be fashion led.

In this, the 6th Volume of the Andrew Martin Interior Design Review, we can see how looks are changing. Harder edgier styles are appearing with echoes of the 60's and 70's. Plastic is back as a design statement. The softer, warmer look that has been so dominant in recent years appears to be on the retreat. But equally again and again minimalism is dismissed as an impractical and unloved fad, which has passed its sell by date. Colour too is mentioned by several designers as overdue for a comeback and a more important element in their work.

The heroes chosen by each designer are an eclectic bunch ranging from Gucci's Tom Ford to the 16th Century Ottoman architect, Sinan. Emile-Jacques Ruhlmann crops up a few times as does Anouska Hempel, but generally they illustrate a huge range of inspiration. This is repeated in the extraordinary diversity of styles, which blend the wishes of the home owner, the personality of the designer, the heritage of the building with the prejudices of fashion. No wonder nobody comes up with quite the same solution.

MARTIN WALLER

amanda rosa interiors

Designer: Amanda Rosa. Company: Amanda Rosa Interiors, Glasgow, UK. Projects: Hotels, including the Malmaison chain, One Devonshire Gardens in Glasgow and the Columbus hotel in Monaco. Plus some residential work and yacht interiors. Home: An Art Deco apartment in Glasgow, a flat in Monaco and searching for land to build a house in France. Heroes: Emile-Jacques Ruhlmann, Anouska Hempel. Inspiration: Art Deco. Love: Good lighting. Loathe: Kitsch.

• I like people to feel good in my spaces so I don't ever want them to be threatening. Ultra-modern hotels can be quite off-putting simply because you're not wearing the right clothes, whereas I want to create instant warmth • I'm not known for using flowers and pattern or mixing masses of different colours that jump up and hit you in the face. Instead I like to be tonal, because for me it's about creating a calm environment, being soft and subtle • I love leather and linens, silks and wool, cashmere - playing with texture rather than pattern • I want to create drama with lighting. In the day it's soft but as it gets darker the drama unfolds and you can pick out a face in a painting.

'You can do any kind of interior but so much depends on how you light it and that gives it its individuality.'

By pinpointing something as simple as a bowl of fruit you make it as important as a sculpture ● One thing I do hate is thin weak furniture with thin weak legs - things that look as though they might fall over if you sneezed. I have quite a masculine approach in that I like things that last and feel solid ● I take my colours from the environment and the mood we're trying to create - whether it's a sexy bar or a fabulously comfortable bedroom. You work around the idea of what you are trying to make someone feel when they walk into that room.

'I love symmetry in the plan of a room and things being lined up.'

• A hotel should flow well and hold together so you know where you are going quite naturally. I don't like bitty hotels where you walk into one little area and it's a different feel to another • When we go away to a hotel we want to be excited but we also want to relax because life is so frantic. The hotel I tend to talk about is The Point in New York State, a series of log cabins, which is so different from anything else. But also the Amanjena in Marrakech is wonderfully tranquil and very Zen-like • A hotel shouldn't be just a home from home and certainly designing a hotel is different to residential work. A hotel should be an experience but at the same time it has to be as good as home. You have to feel glad to be there.

'When something as ordinary as a flower is pinpointed with light then it becomes extraordinary.'

stefan antoni architects

Designer: Stefan Antoni. **Company:** Stefan Antoni Architects, Cape Town, South Africa. **Projects:** Private homes, hotels and restaurants, in South Africa, Spain and New York. **Home:** A house in Cape Town. **Heroes:** Sir Norman Foster, Le Corbusier and Carlo Scarpa. **Inspiration:** Contemporary life. **Love:** A simple, strong space. **Loathe:** Confusion.

• Cape Town is a remarkable city, so close to the sea, the mountains and the countryside. That really affects the way that we approach design. Nature has some incredible lessons to offer • In Cape Town especially the lifestyle is very much indoor outdoor. We are blurring the edges between the two • We'll design sliding glass doors and windows that disappear into cavities, so that even if you are in the house you'll have a strong feeling of the outside. And when you step outside you're still in a highly controlled, designed environment • We are lucky in often creating the architecture of a home first. The architecture and interior design balance each other rather than compete • The union between architecture and interior design should be natural. You shouldn't have

a situation where the architect completes his work and the interior designer then takes over. It has to be an overall process ● There's a rivalry between architects and interior designers. But interiors require you to be so sophisticated these days that to achieve that you need a common vision between architect and interior designer ● I feel more comfortable with the contemporary world.

'Decoration is almost overtaking fashion now as the most exciting aspect of our lifestyles.'

I don't understand classical architecture well enough. It still inspires me but our focus is on more immediate design and architecture ◉ Initially we'll try and design as little as possible into a space. Sometimes we'll end up with too much and have to begin removing elements. The art is knowing when it's just right ◉ We have a lot of very good crafts people with traditional skills - people who know how to apply mud wall finishes, great ceramicists. We're introducing these skills more and more into our work. There is something of a revival in traditional skills.

heiberg cummings design

Designers: William Cummings, Bernt Heiberg, Vibeke Arstal Johansen, Vigdis Kaasa Høegh. **Company:** Heiberg Cummings Design, Oslo, Norway and New York, USA. **Projects:** Residential, restaurants and hotel projects in Europe and the United States. **Home:** Apartment in New York. **Heroes:** Antonio Gaudi and the American architect Graham Gund. **Inspiration:** Travel and classical Scandinavian design. **Love:** Classical patterns, textures and earth colours. **Loathe:** Over coordinated, matching colours

• Our style is post-modern and takes most of its design influences from Scandinavian history and culture, especially 18th century Scandinavian design • We are taking ornament back into design, using basic woods and natural elements, but our interiors are contemporary in their function and suit how people live today • We have been experimenting with colours, but the thread that holds these colours together is the earthy pigment in the paints we use • A transatlantic flavour has crept into our work over recent years, since we've been working in the States. What we do in America has been modified with ideas of comfort and livability - functional ideas rather than stylistic ones • Our American clients do demand more creature comforts, more home technology, which we have responded to. But we also find there's an increasing appeal for that in Europe • We've just opened a furniture

'I think what we do is more timeless than fashionable. But we are trying to be innovative, doing things in a new way, even though we are updating historical influences.'

showroom in New York, showing our own designs. It came about because we were designing individual pieces of furniture for projects and over the years built up a library of designs ● Our furniture uses a lot of solid woods and building techniques from 200 years ago. But we're creating more contemporary objects that suit modern life, not simply reproducing old pieces of furniture ● We've just done a dining table that is very classical in its appearance, but is built at a height where you sit around it with bar stools. It can be used as a work table or a dining table, but takes everything up to a higher level ● I do believe modernism as a style is finished and that people are looking to have history, culture and life back in their homes. Modernism minimalised life to the point where it was beautiful to look at, but lacked a human touch ● Our work is a reaction to modernism. People are still building in a minimalist style all the time because that is the status quo, it is the design establishment today. We are breaking away from that.

'It's about taking very old ideas and putting them in a contemporary setting and showing how they adapt to life today.'

'It's down to the designer to make sure that harmony is found between the old and the new.'

clifton property developments

Designer: Paul Van Geens. **Company:** Clifton Property Developments, London, UK. **Projects:** Mostly large houses in central London, both developments and private design commissions. **Home:** A period house in Chelsea, London. **Heroes:** Frank Lloyd Wright, Sir Norman Foster. **Inspiration:** Architecture. **Love:** Simplicity. **Loathe:** Over complexity, florals, chintz, bureaucracy.

● I'm architecturally led rather than interior design led. I'm very much into the creation of space and how that space is divided up prior to the interior design element of a job ● We work with many listed period properties where there are limits as to what can be done externally. Sometimes we can add an extra floor or dig out the garden, put in a home cinema and then put the garden back on top ● The current fashion in many large houses is to create kitchen, dining and family rooms on the lower ground floor. Some family rooms are doubling as home entertainment centres, with projection screens hidden into ceiling recesses ● Often period buildings with tall ceilings and good proportions offer a better blank canvas to work with than a more modern building ● Maintaining and renovating an old property with period features and mixing an element of modern and contemporary design is a particular pleasure ● Home technology is becoming increasingly important, hidden and unobtrusive but quietly making our lives easier ● Technology has also changed bathrooms. With modern heating and ventilation mirrors don't steam up and condensation doesn't exist. Bathing traditions are also changing with more people requesting showers and wet rooms are becoming increasingly popular. ● We incorporate period antiques and furniture with contemporary design. Most of our clients have objects they treasure and they often ask us to find a place for them in their new scheme.

'We tend to create a blank canvas using neutral tones and then add layers on to the scheme afterwards.'

serdar gülgün

Designer: Serdar Gülgün. **Company:** Serdar Gülgün, Istanbul, Turkey. **Projects:** Private homes, art exhibitions and textile designs. **Home:** An apartment in a 19th century building in Istanbul. **Hero:** Sinan, the great Ottoman architect of the 16th century. **Inspiration:** Ottoman textiles and art. **Love:** Large, deep, low sofas draped with Turkish fabrics. **Loathe:** Cheap theatricality.

• I am an Ottoman art expert by definition. I advise people on forming and organising collections of Ottoman art which then led me into interior decoration as well. But my point of departure is always Ottoman art and fabrics • I believe you should live with artworks and antiques, rather than displaying them behind glass. I love to see things like this used on a daily basis, to touch them and to live with them • I hate display cases - I never use them. If you are afraid of damaging something valuable when it's in your home, you should never get it in the first place. You will be more comfortable without it • In a traditional Ottoman house there wasn't much furniture. You had the building itself, with painted ceilings and walls, and then the fabrics. No sofas or armchairs, but beautiful cushions - the textiles were a central part of the design.

'Minimalism means taking a house and removing the most essential things from it.'

● We may use plainer, more contemporary textiles for a backdrop but the older Ottoman textiles that I bring in for everyday use - cushions, upholstery and so on - tend to be 18th or 19th century. My favourite period in Ottoman history is the 16th century, the reign of Suleiman when the Empire was at its most splendid. But 16th century pieces are rare, so 16th or 17th century Ottoman textiles might now be hung on the wall as panels ● We are not reproducing traditional interiors, piece by piece. There has to be an element of today, as well as a sense of

character and personality that comes from the owner of the house ● I love homes with a sense of humour. So putting in something contemporary or something which forms an opposite to traditional Ottoman design adds a certain charm or element of humour, perhaps something eccentric and idiosyncratic ● The most beautifully designed modern pieces are based on an understanding of classical design and these pieces melt into an interior which mixes the old and new ● When you enter a house you have to feel a sense of who lives in it and also a sense of place and culture - whether it's Istanbul, London, Tokyo, Jaipur. I don't like characterless, anonymous interiors which could just be anywhere in the world.

'Interior design for me comes out of collecting, which gives a character to the house, and provides something you can plan the interior design around.'

richard daniels design

Designer: Richard Daniels. **Company:** Richard Daniels Design, London, UK. **Projects:** Hotel and restaurant design work, including the Bristol Hotel in Warsaw, Lucknam Park in Wiltshire, the Eden Hotel in Rome and the Amigo Hotel in Brussels. Plus occasional residential commissions. **Home:** A house in Putney and a home in Northern France. **Heroes:** Le Corbusier, Frank Lloyd Wright and Andreé Putman. **Inspiration:** Architecture, travel and the Arts. **Love:** Clean interiors with natural materials, neutral colours. **Loathe:** Ostentatious or pretentious spaces.

'We work very much in the contemporary end as well as landmark buildings historically, but we don't let them intimidate us.'

• I am a great believer in the integrity of a building and that you have to start with the planning aspects of a space. This is where we differ from many interior designers - we're really interior architects • We get the integrity of the space right and then drop in things that relate to it, plus a little bit of theatre. When we design a bar or restaurant, we're trying to create an ambience suited to enjoyment and pleasure • It's about respecting the architectural qualities of a building without letting them overwhelm you. We like to bring in a contemporary edge without creating a conflict.

'It's about that little twist of lemon that can make the difference between a bland space and a space with real ambience.'

● With the Eden in Rome, although it had been built in 1889, it had been completely ruined inside. So we really reinvented the space, while acknowledging some of the 1889 history of the building ● Projects like the Eden, the Bristol or the Waldorf Astoria are great to be involved in because they do have a history to their architecture and place in society. Also we need projects that keep us alive, rather than repeating ideas again and again ● Personally I'm very comfortable with Georgian style architecture and Palladian buildings, where the proportions are so well considered ● Designing a hotel now is rather like designing a village or a town. There's every aspect: restaurants, bars, spas, gyms, suites. There's quite a palette of design opportunities.

'I have this need to see order
in the things that I do.'

'People are bored of the simple base c to be more a

aesthetic design is an important a
generally is quite clean but we have
say for powder rooms where we r
paper on the walls. We'll use wallpa
putting in under floor heating for
because we love natural stone floor
if you don't do something about it.

• There's a lot of emphasis on bathrooms now and we're taking a more holistic approach. Gone are the days where the hotel bathroom was a little shoe box. We are almost approaching the hotel room as if it were a pied a terre • From a hoteliers point of view, spas can make a real difference to bookings so we're working on new spas for hotels like Lucknam Park in Wiltshire. There's a great emphasis on spas as part of the whole hotel experience • There's an Eastern influence to some of the spa work we're doing which we are comfortable with because it's simplifying the elements involved. It's much more natural, almost 'spiritual'.

'I don't like things that scream.'

trendson interieur

Designers: Koen and Suzy Van Gestel Clé. **Company:** Trendson Interieur, Mechelen, Belgium. **Projects:** Private houses and apartments. **Home:** A house in Mechelen. **Heroes:** Jacques Garcia and Alberto Pinto. **Inspiration:** Books, magazines. **Love:** Moorish style. **Loathe:** Synthetic fabrics.

• The design of our house and showroom is very eclectic. It's our home but also a presentation of a range of styles, a way to show clients different ideas. But we do prefer it when you can create different atmospheres in one home • The house was once a monastery with parts dating back to 1650, but it has been added to and altered many times over the centuries • Some of the rooms

were designed around a specific thing. The black living room was planned
around some prints we bought in Paris. That was the starting point. But the
starting point can be very different, depending on the room ❋ In a modern
open plan house it's very hard to create different moods. But in a house like

'We like to try and create some drama, a little piece of theatre, in a room.'

ours, where there are many small rooms and hallways, it's easier to create different styles and ambiences within one home ● We like to mix patterns and fabrics, although in Belgium that kind of boldness in a room is quite rare. Many people don't like to take any risks but in our work we like to shake ideas up, to inspire someone to do something different ● Our work is not necessarily a reaction to minimalism because some of our work can involve quite modern, understated spaces. But that's not really our own taste. We prefer something richer, more dramatic ● In Belgium people tend to create a large open-plan living room. They tend to be limited in colour choices because they are living in just one space and opt for calm, neutral colours.

But the colours we like are ox-blood reds, aubergine or black ● We like Moorish style, a Spanish and North African influence, and trying to create something quite eclectic. In the hallway of our home we have a Fortuny-inspired corner and that has a very Moorish atmosphere ● Our furniture is all new, rather than antique. We source furniture and design our own built-in furniture. But the furniture that we like has a traditional basis to the design ● A lot of people are playing too safe with their homes, as well as following fashion too much and creating spaces that date in two or three years. We want to invent something that's beyond fashion and more timeless.

lifestyles interiors

Designer: Helen Green. Company: Lifestyles Interiors, London, UK. Projects: Mainly residential, including show homes, plus a hotel project in Barbados. Home: Georgian house in Chelsea, London. Heroes: Givenchy, Christian Dior. Inspiration: Palladian style. Love: Contrasting textures. Loathe: Exposed lamp wires, fussy flowers.

• Our work is sharp and classical, but incorporating many contemporary materials. So we might have a classical bergère chair in wenge or chocolate stained timber upholstered in a plain contemporary fabric. It's updated classicism • We are experimenting much more with colour now. So we're using amber, orange, crushed raspberry but mostly in upholstery, cushions or glassware • We are using a lot of mirror, both as a way of refracting light and making a room's proportions appear larger than they really are • I'm a great believer in new scene-set lighting systems, which create variable moods in a room. They are preprogrammed to create a whole range of ambient moods. Everyone wants more out of lighting now • Combining modern systems like air conditioning, music, home cinema and lighting with a clean

'We use a lot of hard
natural surfaces, ston
and wood, and ideally
combination of the two

pia maria schmid architecture & design

Designer: Pia Maria Schmid. **Company:** Pia Maria Schmid Architecture & Design, Zurich, Switzerland. **Projects:** Private houses, hotels, restaurants and shops. **Home:** A house in Zurich. **Heroes:** Jean Nouvel, James Turelle. **Inspiration:** Everyday life and everything. **Love:** Olive wood and other heavy, dark woods and rich fabrics. **Loathe:** Nothing. Choices of materials, colours and fabrics just depend on the mix within a scheme.

● I'm open to every material. It just depends on where, how and in which way you're using it and how it mixes in with other things. The same is true of my attitude to colours ● My style is very expressive, instinctive and extravagant but also analytical. I do like to pare things

down, but at the moment I am using some baroque elements. So there's a mix of old and new ● I like to think that I am always heading forwards, from the present into the future. But I also include good and lasting elements of traditional artwork and furniture ● At the moment I'm working on hotel projects in Switzerland and Berlin, where I'm designing a new hotel in the old Siemens factory. With both, the challenge lies in keeping the facades of these historic buildings while creating very modern interiors ● It's important to understand the relationship between the exterior and interior. The two should go together, not be seen as completely separate entities. For the future, I want to experiment more with creating an almost seamless transition between inside and out ● When I'm starting a project I have to analyse every aspect of it. I need to learn as much as possible about the building, the brief, the clients, before I can even start designing ● Too many designers are just looking at design magazines and copying what they see. It's far more important to use your own ideas, express your own originality and individuality and find the source of your inspiration.

'Designers have to find their own direction, to set their own agenda.'

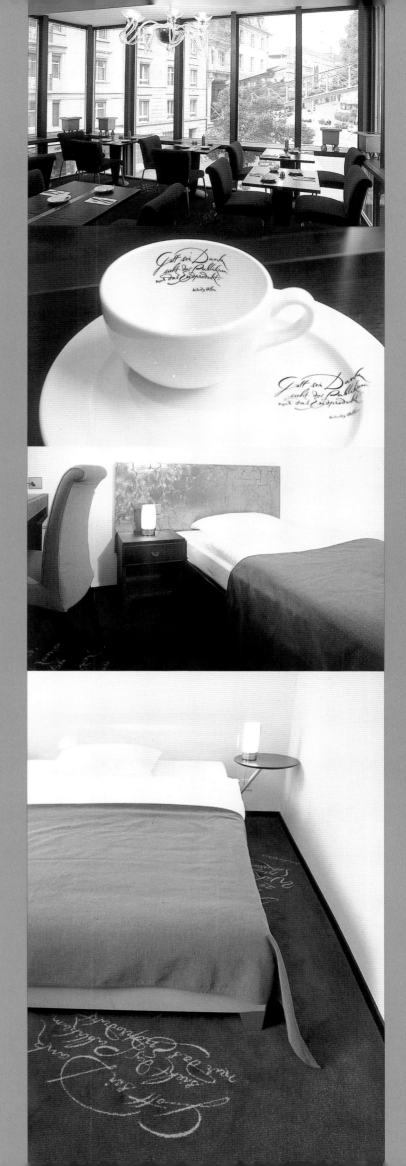

anna bilton design

Designer: Anna Bilton. Company: Anna Bilton Design, London, UK. Projects: Private residential houses and apartments, plus show apartments. Home: Contemporary terraced home in Belgravia, London. Heroes: Zaha Hadid, Matthew Hilton, Eva Jiricna. Inspiration: Different textures. Love: Limestone. Loathe: Shag pile.

● I try to draw on whatever the client has, whether it's a painting, a piece of furniture, or something else that's special to them. Then I try to design a room around that one piece ● I like the juxtaposition of antique and contemporary furniture. It's often possible to complement a period piece with something very modern. I dc prefer contemporary design, but I'm not prejudiced against antiques ● The last project we did was a church conversion and there we put in a mirror going right into the water of a

'Texture is really where I start from. I like contrasting texture, such as velvet with raffia, leather with silk.'

swimming pool. It was a size issue, and we needed a wow factor that basically made the space look twice the size it really was ● Another thing that worked very well was using etched glass and clever lighting for a shower cubicle, so you could just see the silhouette of the person showering ● I'm not theatrical in the sense that I use lots of gilt and fabric but I do like the sense of being able to look at something and say that really is amazing. I like impactive spaces and playing with scale, such as oversizing a fireplace in a room

• Communication technology is paramount, with so many people working from home and it's very important in a home office to build in all the technology that they will need • I incorporate some Eastern, African or South American elements into my work. I like to bring a non-European element into an interior that's very westernised. I'll use it as an accent in a room rather than the basis of it • I did a project where I brought a series of sculptural pieces from Africa and put them across a wall in a very dark room. There

was nothing else that was African so they really stood out • I take quite a lot of inspiration from fashion design, looking at the colour palettes which come across and into the home. Neutrals will always be there, but at the moment I love deep purples and rich chocolate browns • I tend to mix my own paint colours rather than buying them from a chart. In the church conversion it looks on first impression as though there's the same neutral colour throughout, but actually there's nine different shades.

kit kemp

Designer: Kit Kemp. **Company:** Firmdale Hotels, London, UK. **Projects:** Hotel projects including the Covent Garden Hotel and the recent Charlotte Street Hotel, plus occasional private commissions. **Home:** A London house and a country home in Hampshire. **Hero:** Frank Gehry. **Inspiration:** Nature. **Love:** Natural surfaces - stone, wood, verdigris. **Loathe:** Highly moulded plastics.

• Often we're working with buildings that don't offer much inspiration, for instance one was an old dental warehouse and one was a hospital. So you're creating an environment from scratch • With our interiors, we're talking about rooms that never even existed before. So we are trying to create a space that looks spontaneous and easy yet the only way to do that is with an

enormous amount of planning ● People probably come in to the hotels and say 'oh well, the designer hasn't done anything here at all'. That's great if they think that. There's a lot of artifice to designing a hotel, but it has to look artless ● If somewhere looks too contrived, it doesn't actually work. It has to look inspiring and fun and make you wander around and feel good ● You do have to be aware of the need for materials to last in a hotel. You can't put very fine silks on a chair that will look great

'The bad points of a building have to be turned around and turned into something positive.'

but just for five minutes. That's a consideration, but it's not constricting. It's just part of getting things to work ● Because Charlotte Street is near Bloomsbury it was easy to think of bringing in that influence. But people like Duncan Grant also loved things that were contemporary, so I didn't want a pastiche of the past but something with many different things brought in ● Within every century there's different aspects of design that are fascinating and that's why you become an interior designer, because you don't like one thing. You like loads of things and seeing them done well ● We design and

make all our furniture. It's based on traditional lines but everything is made to our specification and that's a very interesting part of the job. They have very English references and are very solid - oak, ash, solid woods ● With the cinema we've done at Charlotte Street there would have been no point unless it was state of the art technically. But if it looks nice as well that's great, with grey pinstripe on the walls and orange leather seats, which smell lovely ● I'm anti-international. Our hotels are definitely English and of their place. If you are coming from abroad our hotels seem to be what people want because they do have a very English character.

'I like minimalism, but it's far too serious. You should be able to smile.'

joanna trading

Designer: Joanna Wood. **Company:** Joanna Trading, London, UK. **Projects:** Residential work in UK, Europe, USA, Scandinavia, plus specialist hotel projects and select commercial spaces such as executive offices. **Home:** A Georgian house in Belgravia, London. **Heroes:** Sir John Soane, John Fowler and David Hicks. **Inspiration:** Travelling, most recently in China. **Love:** Comfort. **Loathe:** Furniture at angles across the corners of rooms, yellow lamp shades.

● Our style has been called 'new traditional'. But I have always had quite plain taste and so 'traditional', for me, doesn't mean that you have to throw every antique piece that you've got into a room ● Is it comfortable, is it practical, does it actually work? These are the criteria by which I judge everything, whether it's a zen guest cottage or a farmhouse in Provence ● Minimalism for me does not work. It's rather like the emperor's new clothes. You try having friends and family to stay, or working and entertaining in a space with one hard surface and an orchid. It just doesn't work ● As a company we're very good at the whole picture from architecture through to the last lamp shade, the last detail. There is no division as far as I'm concerned - one does not exist without

the other ● I like early Georgian style - George I and George II - where the clean, simple lines can often look very contemporary. But at the moment I'm doing a house inspired by the 1930s and I'm also loving working with that ● The way we're projecting television now is exciting and wherever possible we're using flat screens. The way we're handling news and information in the home now is fascinating ● Glass is being used very structurally now. In a penthouse we've just done we used ceiling hung panels of glass to demark two areas. That had a wonderful lightness to it without interrupting the views or the light ● I love glass that has a wonderful green tinge to it, using it a little bit deeper than normal so it comes up a little bit greener ● Many people just don't know how to finish things off. I hate bathrooms that

'If you're given a Frank Lloyd Wright building then you wouldn't treat it in the same way as a Vanburgh.'

have got messy grouting. You've got marble, granite or limestone - these beautiful, hard, clean, simple surfaces - which are spoiled by poor finishing ● I have just been to Castle Howard so right now that's my favourite building. But I'm also working on a wooden holiday home on a fjord in Denmark, which couldn't be further away. But I will certainly draw inspiration from that too ● I'm very inspired by set design and I think if I wasn't doing what I do then I would be involved in theatre design, something intricate like that. I've always been fascinated by the juxtaposition of costume to scenery.

Designer: Tara Bernerd. Company: Yoo Too, London, UK. Projects: Developing and designing Yoo Too apartments in Brighton and London, collaborating with Philippe Starck on the London Yoo flats, plus occasional one-off homes. Home: Contemporary apartment in a terraced house in Maida Vale, London. Heroes: Luis Barragan, Tadao Ando and Christian Liaigre. Inspiration: Films and film-making. Love: Old leather club chairs, wide wooden floorboards and juxtaposing something antique with contemporary lines. Loathe: Salmon colours.

● I like to create a feeling of escape, interiors where people can't quite place where they are. I feel I've got there when somebody walks in and says, 'I could be in a totally different country'. That means you've taken somebody away ● I like the idea of discovery, not seeing everything at once. Having gone to film school I look at interiors as though I'm composing a shot. You do see the room as a whole, but it's about creating different compositions within that ● It's certainly an international style. I have travelled a lot and I'm the kind of person who absorbs my surroundings. But you do also tune into every project. I am flexible about the demands of each

'I am a designer but I'm also a creative developer.'

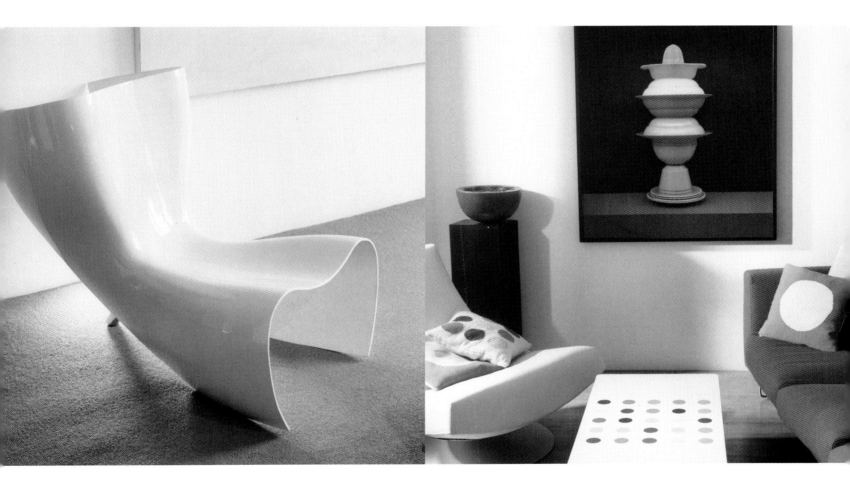

space ● I like building flexibility into living space, with sliding doors and moving walls ● If you've got a two bedroomed apartment, it's hard to say if people will want a second bedroom or use that as a dining room or a workspace. So you have to allow for various different moods and uses. We're now used to a less rigid way of living ● In my own home I used a heavy metal roll down garage door, which slides up into a bulkhead and disappears. Using it involves either guts or madness, but it cuts a large room in half and looks very dramatic. I'll use that idea again ● There's a lot of separated couples, people who might have a current partner, kids, step-children. So you need a second bedroom, but you want the flexibility to section off part of it every now and then for another use, like a home office ● It's nice to have an open plan

'My work is contemporary and simple, not fussy or pretentious, with a richness to the colours.'

kitchen if you don't have a big home, so you can talk to people as you cook. But if you've made a big mess, it's good to then be able to section that off so your kitchen becomes a cool looking screen ● With kitchens, everyone now expects things like a good extractor, microwaves. What's more important in a kitchen than being high-tech is that it's user friendly and really works ergonomically ● People have got to live in a space that works, with good storage, closets, wardrobes. People have stuff and it's got to go somewhere. You have got to imagine someone living there day to day.

hennie interiors

Designer: Helene Forbes Hennie **Company:** Hennie Interiors, Oslo, Norway. **Projects:** Mostly private homes, ski and summer houses, offices, restaurants, hotels. **Home:** A period apartment in Oslo. **Heroes:** John Saladino, Anouska Hempel, Ralph Lauren and Donna Karan. **Inspiration:** Clients, their spaces and the different environments they inhabit. **Love:** Velvet. **Loathe:** Bad lighting.

• Because we have a variety of clients it means we have to be aware of many different styles and periods in design. We don't have one house style, because we would find that too limiting • I was brought up in Norway, but I have also lived abroad and so there are other influences. Sometimes my work is influenced by traditional Scandinavian style, but not too much because I like to experiment • Occasionally we will do something traditional, like the wooden hunting cabin. It's typically Norwegian and there we had to be sympathetic to the building. But at the same time we did a modern apartment with a much more international flavour • The main thing with the cabin

'A good interior architect should have a knowledge of many different styles.'

was that even though we had redesigned it we wanted to make it feel as though it had been that way a long time. We wanted it to feel natural and lived in, which is very important, even in modern spaces ● The setting is very important. One of the best things that we did with the cabin was making sure that you could look through the whole house and out across the countryside. We wanted to make the most of that ● It is true that we will use a lot of natural materials in whatever we do and also aim for a lighter space because of the Scandinavian influence, perhaps more so than designers in other

countries ● We have just decorated an old apartment using antique mirrored panels in the hallway. It makes the apartment feel enormous and creates a very light atmosphere ● I take a lot of pleasure in introducing technology, even into old spaces - TV, music, computers, lighting. It is demanding to build that into a home discreetly and effectively. It has to look as natural as possible ● I have spent a lot of time travelling in Spain, which is a very inspiring country. The textiles, furniture and colours you find there are so interesting and sometimes we bring a little of that Mediterranean flavour into our work.

carter tyberghein

Designers: Laura Carter & Patrick Tyberghein. **Company:** Carter Tyberghein, London, UK. **Projects:** Private homes, show flats and hotels in the UK, France and elsewhere. **Home:** An apartment in London. **Heroes:** Emile-Jacques Ruhlmann and Gae Aulenti. **Inspiration:** The context/environment of any particular project. **Love:** Blood red velvet, matt finishes. **Loathe:** Synthetic finishes, such as fake marble.

● The context and the environment in which we are designing is very important. Depending on whether we are designing on the Continent or working in England, the answer to a problem may be very different ● We're not trying to stamp one look on everything we do, although we have aspirations which are contemporary and eclectic. Yet we will always try to put something of ourselves into what we do ● We bring in a 1930s influence but without it being too obvious. It gives a nice base to the interiors. But 30s style was often strong and austere so we prefer a softer suggestion to what we do ● We've done a hotel in Paris near the Champs Elysees and the French do like a 1930s Deco touch. So we've put a hint of that in but without making it too obvious ● Patrick is French, Laura is English. So it's an Anglo-French alliance, which is a nice combination, bringing in different views and slightly different ways of looking at things ● We source furniture worldwide and design our own furniture, which is made in France. The lines are quite contemporary and simple and the

 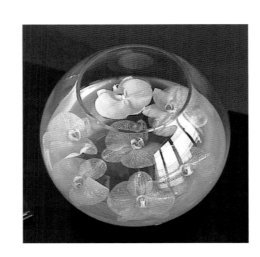

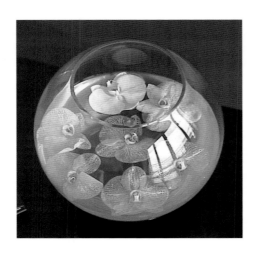 

designs play with texture. But we will mix them in with antique pieces, which is important for us ● Humour is very important - just adding a small touch of humour which makes the interiors stand out. It could be just adding something incongruous on a shelf or a console - a little surprise ● We don't go as far as minimalism - our work is more decorative and opulent than that. Blood reds, for instance, are a strong influence at the moment, even if it's just for accessories or artwork ● In some projects we can go a little wilder and use bold colours, reds on a neutral background, or aubergine accents, or oranges and blues on a neutral backdrop. But when our work has an element of opulence, it's an understated kind of opulence.

walda pairon/giardini

Designer: Walda Pairon. **Company:** Walda Pairon/ Giardini, Heide-Kalmthout, Belgium. **Projects:** Private houses, hotels, garden design. **Home:** An old, renovated house in Belgium. **Hero:** Andrea Palladio. **Inspiration:** Travel. **Love:** Aubergine and rich shades of red. **Loathe:** Synthetic fabrics.

● What I'm working towards is the creation of spaces in which people can feel comfortable and express their individuality. To achieve that, I need to build a relationship with a client and really involve myself in their lives ● I'm not trying to invent interiors which are just my own expression. They have to belong to the clients, the people who are going to live in a house. The interiors should cocoon them naturally because they are modelled on their own personality ● I'm always travelling for my work but rarely consciously searching for specific objects. I just like to browse, wander into local antique shops and see what I can find ● My favourite places are countries which harbour sources of civilisation and culture. Italy is a second home, but I'm also fond of

Spain, England and the great cities of Europe and America ● On a flight over the Grand Canyon, bathed in the red glow of the sun, I found myself inspired for a new collection of fabrics. That's how travel and experience can generate ideas ● I don't let myself be guided by rules in deciding what is beautiful or worthwhile. Sense and sensibility are more important than expertise ● Beauty brings happiness with it: a collection of fabrics in a

'Interior design is an intense form of communication.'

harmony of colours and textures, or using the right combination of beautiful natural materials like wood and stone, can generate an almost sensual sense of pleasure ● When a commission is finished, I often feel empty. I miss the rooms, the people, the objects, that have become so much my own. It's as if I had lost a much-loved person.

'Simplicity is the height of style.'

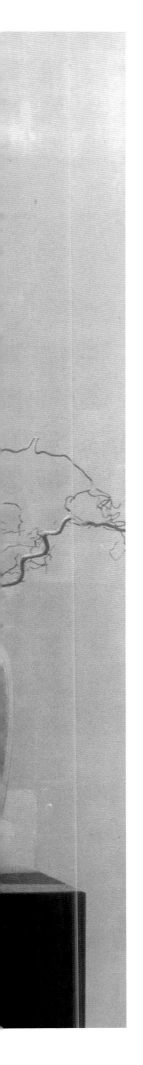

estudio f. interiores

Designer: Jorge Fuentes. **Company:** Estudio F. Interiores, Barcelona, Spain. **Projects:** Residential, restaurants and hotels. **Home:** A house in Barcelona. **Hero:** Jean-Michel Frank. **Inspiration:** Everyday living and unexpected sights. **Love:** Unusual textured materials such as braided leather, parchment, shark skin, eggshell. **Loathe:** Overly flowery fabrics and obvious commercialism.

● I'm not into minimalism - you need things around you to feel comfortable - but my projects are not overdone either. I avoid anything superfluous. My style is sober and sophisticated, with a small 1930s influence which fits in with a contemporary look ● I like to play and experiment rather than getting stuck with just one style. So our work can be rustic, urban, modern, a little more

'We like taking classical techniques and using them to create something more contemporary.'

classical. But always with an emphasis on texture and avoiding excess ● I like unusual textures, like feather lamp shades, and finding very different materials which make you look twice but then make you admit that, yes, it works well. That's one of an interior designer's tasks - to experiment with new ideas ● We play with paint effects, such as the stone effect we used on a recent house project. It's like a sheet of stone, with a texture to it. It's not something classical like trompe l'oeil but more up to date and contemporary in its look ● In the distribution of furniture and the proportion of rooms there is a classical influence to the work. But I also like to break the symmetry every now and then with a surprise, something unexpected which changes the rhythm ● I like to mix modern art with old prints for contrast.

I wouldn't do a whole house with 18th century art, but I like a mix. With furniture too, just one or two special antiques create a different touch and really stand out within a contemporary home ● We work with a lot of neutrals but I don't get stuck on them. For a restaurant we might use brighter colours and more innovative materials, such as metallics like copper. A restaurant can be more of a design statement than a home, so it allows you more leeway to create a different look ● At the moment we are working on restaurants which evolve through the day, using lighting. They change from morning, to lunch, to dinner. I tend to use high tech lighting, systems that shouldn't be obvious when you're in the space itself.

louise bradley

Designer: Louise Bradley. **Company:** Louise Bradley, London, UK. **Projects:** Mainly residential. **Home:** Apartment in a Georgian house, central London. **Hero:** Andrea Palladio. **Inspiration:** Great pieces of 18th and 19th century furniture. **Love:** Stone colours and textures. **Loathe:** Badly made replica furniture.

• My style draws together Spanish, Italian and French pieces in quite a Continental feel. I love the flea markets of Paris or Madrid and scouring the salvage yards for something exciting • A key piece of old furniture, a picture or a mirror can be something I will build a whole room around. It can be quite unusual and unexpected, like an old gate to use as a headboard or an iron grille that could be a radiator cover. It doesn't have to be a fine piece of furniture • Every part of a room should tell its own story, so that when you walk in you should be able to look around, see lots of different pieces, textures and materials, and stay interested • Your carpet or choice of flooring is so important as the base of a room.

Everything else follows from that. It should never be an afterthought but a priority from the very beginning ● I use a very soft palette for the walls and the floors - limestones, creams, natural colours - and then play with colour in accessories, paintings, the frame of a picture ● I never stop looking for antiques and furniture. You constantly need to search for new ideas, new things to feed yourself. Now I've opened an antique shop so when I'm collecting and don't have a home for something then at least it's got somewhere to live.

'I like elaborate pieces in

relatively plain settings.'

'The key thing for me is to define a modern kind of comfort using elements of the classic and the contemporary.'

• I don't hate minimalism. I can appreciate how hard it is to do well because every detail is in on show. When you are really filling a room then at least there are areas the eye isn't drawn to • It's important to play with different heights in a room, not have everything sitting on a table-top level. You need bookcases, shelves, something going on at every level so the eye roams around the room rather than just staying still.

olivier interior design

Designer: François Antoine Olivier **Company:** Olivier Interior Design, Drap, France. **Projects:** Private homes, apartments, boats and clubs, such as the Automobile Club de Monaco. **Home:** A house in the country, near Drap, shared with three dogs. **Heroes:** Too many to list, because each period has its own design heroes. **Inspiration:** A garden, a fragrance, a colour, a town, a film.... **Love:** Perfect lighting. **Loathe:** Rustic style and theatricality.

• I don't like to be categorised in terms of just one style or trend. I like to combine very different things and create a harmony between them. What's most important is to use the materials and colours which suit each individual project • I would not want tc copy a style of decoration or architecture from the past. I prefer to analyse styles and sometimes develop certain details or features that can be adapted to today's interiors • I'm particularly fond of lighting by fibre optics, but I also appreciate real candles on an 18th century

'It's important to avoid self-satisfaction because it paralyses development and kills creativity.'

crystal chandelier ● When I begin a new project it's vital to def.ne the atmosphere which we want to create, depending on who is going to live there. Then comes the choice of colours, materials and furnishing. Finally, but most important, is harnessing the light. Organising the lighting of a home is a highly personal job ● My work is sometimes influenced by places I have visited and appreciated, such as the villas of Pompeii with their frescoes and patios. Or Versailles with its excess, the detail on every square inch, and its refinement ● I prefer colours with depth: the reds you find in Japanese lacquer, bronze greens, ivory, particular shades of grey ● I like to use fabrics that drape well and, for curtains, material which cascades onto the floor in a sculptural way. My favourite fabrics are flannel and muslin, silk taffeta and special cottons ● Touch is very important, especially for upholstery fabric and seating. For seating, I tend to give priority to the material over the design.

société christine gérondeau

Designer: Christine Gérondeau **Company:** Société Christine Gérondeau, Paris, France. **Projects:** Mostly hotels, but also occasional commissions for private homes. **Home:** An apartment in Paris. **Heroes:** Christian Liaigre and Jacques Garcia. **Inspiration:** The historic buildings that we work on and reinterpreting styles from the past, especially the 18th century. **Love:** Harmonising colours. **Loathe:** Pretentious and cluttered interiors.

● Our work is a modern interpretation of period style. So we might have 18th century style armchairs in the lobby of a hotel but combine them with modern fabrics, so as to bring them up to date and make the look a little more informal ● We do sometimes mix antiques with contemporary pieces. I have also designed my own range of furniture and that is contemporary, with a very simple style of design. It incorporates classical influences but in a very modern way ● We very rarely work with new hotels. It's mostly renovations of period buildings, so often there is already an atmosphere to these places which gives us a starting point for our design scheme ● People say that I have a tendency towards masculine interiors, especially in the use of light and colour. Certainly, I don't like a light style of decoration ● We recently worked

'In terms of design, hoteliers are more concerned now with comfort and giving their guests more choice rather than decoration purely as decoration.'

on the Hotel Baltimore, a four star hotel in Paris. The building is 18th century and very classical. The look was very traditional before but we have now created something relaxed and contemporary ● At the Baltimore, three quarters of the clients are businessmen so we designed a more masculine look. For instance, many of the fabrics that we used are similar to those for men's suits, very tailored and simple ● Hoteliers are also asking for more individual looks for bedrooms. In The Baltimore, for instance, which has 105 rooms, Sofitel wanted five different designs for the bedrooms rather than perhaps two before, to give guests more choice ● I'm very sensitive to colours. I like subtle harmonies. I prefer subtle tones, but with just a touch of glitter. It's about creating variations of colours in a similar spectrum but with one touch of sharpness or brightness that really stands out ● Mixing colours within a space is like making a sauce when you're cooking. There's a moment when the balance is just right and to add anything else would be to ruin it ● My definition of a good home is a place where you can feel comfortable, where the furniture and objects feel naturally placed, somewhere where you can feel the personality of the people who live there.

candy and candy

Designers: Nicholas Candy and Christian Candy. **Company:** Candy and Candy, London, UK. **Projects:** Mostly residential - houses, apartments, luxury developments - plus a hotel project. **Home:** A home in Belgravia, London (Nicholas) and a penthouse in Berkeley Square, London (Christian). **Hero:** Thierry Despont. **Inspiration:** Travel and fashion. **Love:** Alcantara. **Loathe:** Cheap imitations of anything.

• We try to combine influences from lots of different cultures and mix them with contemporary fabrics and styles. And we design a lot of our furniture, much of which will use a lot of classical principles but with a modern feel • We tend to work mainly with Grade I or Grade II listed period buildings which are very traditional in nature, but we'll bring in a modern influence and bring them right up to date • We're very influenced by high technology: plasma screens, fingerprint door entry, drop down cinema

screens. In our spaces any telephone can control the music, TV and intercom systems ● We always take out all the old electrics and totally rewire the entire space. Even if the technology of handsets or whatever it may be moves on they can easily be upgraded, because it's the labyrinth of wires behind the wall that is important ● We've developed an idea which means every room can have a control panel with a floor plan of the apartment to adjust all the blinds, curtains, lighting, TV, stereo, from wherever you are in the home. A lot of our technology is bespoke ● In one project we're putting in a steel reinforced, air conditioned room just for art. So instead of having your art with a storage company you can have it in a dedicated totally secure room within your apartment ● Our clients want laundry rooms and even ironing rooms, as well as the kitchen and utility room. Instead of four guest bedrooms, these days people want more space for themselves and perhaps just two guest bedrooms ● Some of the things we're now putting into kitchens include champagne fridges, American-style fridge

'A home should be more than comfortable, it should be intimate.'

freezers, microwaves and cappuccino machines as standard. These are all standard for us now ● For several years we tended to keep colours fairly simple, soft and neutral, but now we're moving away from that towards a greater mix of colours with darker, richer tones and some bolder colours ● We bring senses alive by mixing textures like marble, rare woods, cashmere, silks and linen. It makes you want to look, touch, feel and enjoy.

'It's all about creating a lifestyle and a way of living.'

head interiors

Designers: Sharon Fihrer and Michael Harrison. **Company:** Head Interiors, Johannesburg, South Africa. **Projects:** Residential, retail and high end corporate work in South Africa and UK. **Home:** A modern house in Johannesburg. **Heroes:** John Stefanidis, Anouska Hempel and Billy Baldwin. **Inspiration:** Africa and travel. **Love:** Basketware. **Loathe:** Over-decorated rooms.

• There's a quote of Billy Baldwin's that we think about all the time: 'comfort is the ultimate luxury'. Comfort is very important to us within a home • We like to know what's going in the world and spend a lot of time in Europe especially, but living in Africa gives us a lot of energy and part of our success is combining the African and European influence • Our colour palette and choice of materials is greatly influenced by being in Africa. The light is very different here and that gives you a different perspective. During the day we are flooded with light and live in very light, bright surroundings • In our design work we are constantly looking at African materials - the timber, the beadwork, the metalwork, wire baskets. But we will bring those things up to date, make it a little more sophisticated • We think we're at a great advantage because we live in Africa, but

'What we are really doing in a space is layering, which really comes out of fashion design.'

we're able to travel easily to France, Italy and England and bring back ideas and materials. We bring in an eclectic mix from many different avenues ● People spend a lot of time in their offices and many of them have become more like a study - a softer, more comfortable space. And more people have an office at home now, with all that involves. So there's a healthy cross-over there ● In a city like London you're always looking inside, but in South Africa there are few houses that don't lead you to the outside. For much of the year you are living outdoors and so outside living space has to be integral ● Having a retail side that's always developing merchandise, we've just designed a range of furniture made to be used both indoors and out and to move between the two. It's about making connections between indoors and out.

'We create retro classic functional interiors that revolve around a comfortable lifestyle.'

homeira interior design

Designer: Homeira Pour Heidari. Company: Homeira Interior Design, Munich, Germany. Projects: Mostly private homes in Germany, Italy, Austria, Switzerland, England and America, but also commercial work. Home: An apartment in Munich. Hero: Anouska Hempel. Inspiration: Experiences of having lived in Persia, Canada, America, London and now Germany. Love: Natural colours, greys, browns, taupes and off-whites. Loathe: Lack of attention to detail, bad lighting, cold interiors without soul.

● I grew up in Persia until the age of eight and then I lived in Canada, the US, London, Germany. I have also travelled a lot in India, South Africa, Morocco and Europe. This background, in such different places, is important to me and my work ● The way you work is an expression of your personality. My personality is a mixture of all the cultures I've got to know and I love to mix these different styles ● The Persian influence really comes through in a mood - an element of the romantic. Sometimes there will be one or two pieces from Persia as well - perhaps an antique silver box or something like that ● My work is not actually very Oriental

stylistically, but more European or international in terms of colours, fabrics and materials • I'm just doing a Bavarian house in traditional Bavarian style, but the clients want some more modern pieces, so it's an opportunity to bring in these international influences and bring it up to date • I do tend to use some simple antiques - especially Art Deco and Biedermeier - combined with modern furniture. I will just use one or two pieces that really catch the eye • I give people the chance to have chameleon-like

'You have to be able to understand what your client wants but you also have to be able to place your signature on what you do.'

'When you have lived in different cultures you see things differently.'

rooms where the design of the space allows you to have a light, bright look in summer. But then in winter you can create another, cosier mood within the same interior by changing the accessories ● There's a flexibility to this kind of interior design which is what people are saying they want. It means that you use neutral colours for the basis of the space, but then add different colours with cushions and throws ● Design trends change very quickly now and people get bored with a look. But you can't throw your sofa out of your house after six months. With a strong base to a room you can easily create a different atmosphere without doing too much.

françois champsaur

Designer: François Champsaur. Company: François Champsaur, Paris, France. Projects: Private houses and apartments, hotels, restaurants and boutiques. Home: A farmhouse in Provence. Heroes: David Hockney and photographer Thomas Dernand. Inspiration: Rural architecture. Love: Untreated raw woods. Loathe: Anything fake, false or synthetic.

• The influences on my work are very diverse. There are no restrictions • I would describe myself as working within a contemporary style, but with a strong emphasis on the quality and richness of the materials • I prefer to use natural materials and fabrics in cohesive colours, but then I add in accessories in different, contrasting tones • With many interior design projects, I also design most of the furniture for the house so everything fits together - the structural work, the decoration, the furniture • Location and a sense of place - the environment which surrounds a house or a hotel - are very important in developing a design which suits its surroundings. It's bringing something up to date but with care • I would say my speciality is creating and developing a look for a space through furniture, colours, fabrics - many different things - without losing the

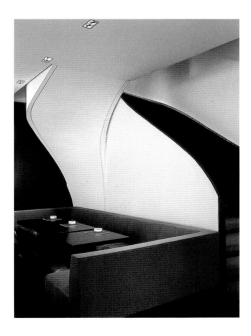

'I like working on projects which are sophisticated in their treatment of light.'

essential spirit and feeling of a building ● With some projects, you need to really go back to the origins of the house, the original conception and structure of the building, before you can bring it into the 21st century and make it work for today ● You have to talk to your clients, to understand how they are going to live in a space and imagine how you can really make it work for them. You have to form a relationship and know what they like and what they don't ● It's a mistake to think more about designing according to fashion, or fitting into a trend, than concentrating on the art of living itself - the necessities and pleasures of day to day to life. That's what our work has to be about ● As a designer you have to be curious all the time and interested in everything. Your eyes have to be open all the time, to contemporary art, photography, the countryside around you, cooking…. Everything.

hecker phelan

Designers: Paul Hecker & Kerry Phelan. **Company:** Hecker Phelan, Victoria, Australia. **Projects:** Private homes, restaurants and clubs. **Home:** A house in Victoria. **Heroes:** Marc Newson, Tom Ford. **Inspiration:** The media, fashion design and fashion magazines. **Love:** Mirrors. **Loathe:** Marine plywood joinery, aluminium look laminate and cheap synthetic materials.

• We start from a very simple architectural basis. It's clean and modernist in the sense of its simplicity and the quality of materials that we use. Then we layer on top of that and it becomes a question of how heavily we'll add in those layers • The Establishment is a new leisure and hotel complex in Sydney, in a 19th century building, where we designed the public spaces - restaurants, bars, night-club. Our interiors are very modern but some historical details were reinstated • On the ground floor there is a huge bar, with a garden, and another bar opening onto the road. In that instance it was all about bringing people off the street and into the space so there was a very strong connection between inside and out • One way that we loosely connected all of our areas at The Establishment was using the thematic idea of a chandelier. Sometimes it would be something very

'Our approach is modernist initially and then there's a layering which makes the interiors more complex.'

contemporary as in the bars and sometimes more traditional, as in the restaurant ● It is important to have a sense of play and fun. Where you have to be careful is that it doesn't become whimsical or trite. You have to have fun in a very sophisticated way ● With bars, you know they have a lifespan and will be redone in four years time. So you have the luxury of being experimental. What you want to do is to achieve a level of quality

and sophistication in the design and then you can have some fun ● Our basic palette of materials is simple. At the moment we're into silver travertine, terrazzo, mirror glass.... Mirror glass can be a very unexpected material and just now we're experimenting with mirrors sitting against mirrored walls ● The easiest thing is to do a beautiful white interior, white walls and floors, put some techno furniture into it, and that's that. The test comes when you push yourself out of your comfort zone and start to experiment.

'You have to keep changing and developing to keep the things fun. There's no point in remaining static.'

taylor howes designs

Designers: Karen Howes and Gail Taylor. Company: Taylor Howes Designs, London, UK. Projects: Mainly residential, also show apartments, hotels, health spas. Home: An atelier in a riverside development in Battersea (Karen Howes) and a period house in Westbourne Grove (Gail Taylor). Heroes: Mary Fox Linton, David Hicks. Inspiration: Fashion design and travel. Love: Quality, great craftsmanship. Loathe: Fussiness, pretension.

● We're reinventing traditional influences but with a contemporary twist. Our themes are strong, but also calming and uncluttered. There's a focus on feature furniture, figurative art, sculpture and layered texture ● The Eastern influence is there, but there's also an African flavour coming in with some of the feel of a safari lodge. You can have those different influences working harmoniously in one home. Not everything has to be Chinese or South African ● People can live with antiques in a very modern development. We tend not to overfill a space like that, but underfill it with really exceptional pieces ● Red is one of our favourite colours that we come back to again and again. While we will aim for a calm

'How you balance the new and the old is a real challenge for a designer.'

environment overall - using a lot of whites and creams - we're also aiming for something stimulating and uplifting ● We're trying to create calm retreats in a mad world. Kitchens used to be a big priority, but at the moment it's bathrooms or spa bathrooms. It used to be home gyms, but now it's meditation rooms and reading dens ● Open planning in terms of the main living space will be around for some time to come, yet we're finding very few people who need 4 or 5 bedrooms, so those spare rooms are being turned

'We're very symmetrical people. We love balance.'

into a study or a library ● Bathrooms are the retreat within the retreat. The proportion of the rooms themselves are bigger and a lot more is going into the bathrooms, like walk-in steam showers and good storage facilities to get rid of clutter ● In some projects we'll have his bathroom and her bathroom, his dressing room and hers, creating areas of personal space. And materials tend to be very natural - wood and stone - often with some of the feeling of an oriental spa ● In a recent penthouse we did we had an internal garden, playing with the idea of inside/outside space, and lightly enclosed and

DAVID BAILEY ARCHIVE ONE

PETER LINDBERGH

protected by glass walls ● Getting staircases right is very important as they are often such visible parts of the home. We're just doing one at the moment using steel, wood, glass and leather so it will be a real focal point. It's a work of art in its own right.

joao mansur
architecture & design

Designer: Joao Mansur. **Company:** Joao Mansur Architecture & Design, Sao Paolo, Brazil. **Projects:** Private homes, restaurants, nightclubs, shops, hotels. **Home:** A penthouse in a neoclassical style building in Sao Paolo. **Heroes:** Andrea Palladio, Mies van der Rohe, David Hicks. **Inspiration:** Palladian classicism and Bauhaus. **Love:** Black and white for colour and velvet, silk and leather. **Loathe:** Lilac and citrus colours.

● My style is essentially classical, but with touches of modernity. The classical influence comes through in my approach to symmetry, proportion and an emphasis on strong architectural elements ● To my mind the most common mistakes in interior design are a poor sense of proportion and bad lighting. But superfluous detail is also a mistake ● I was born in Rio de Janeiro, which was the centre of Brazil under the Empire and the capital of the Republic. So there were very international references and a strong Portuguese influence which comes through in my style ● A timeless East meets West theme is also

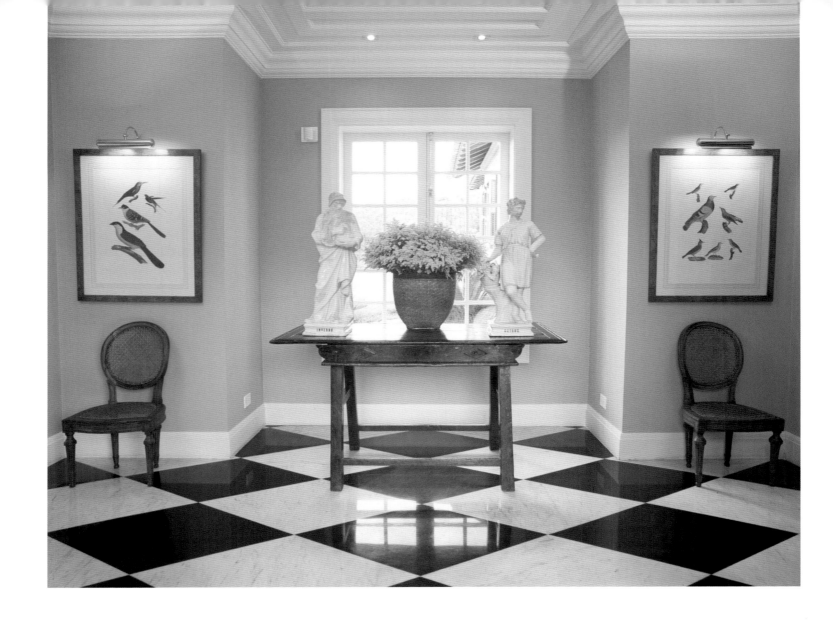

evident in my work, where European antiques blend with Oriental pieces such as rugs, screens and ceramics. That was something you often found in the old houses of Rio during my childhood ● I love to mix the old and new - it's the base for my interiors. But there are no rules as far as linking the two are concerned. You must have courage and a certain sensibility to play with the balance between new and old ● One recent residential project was a huge apartment in a building with a classical French atmosphere. I was

'It's important for a designer to be aware of new trends, new ideas, without ever losing the essence of their own individual style.'

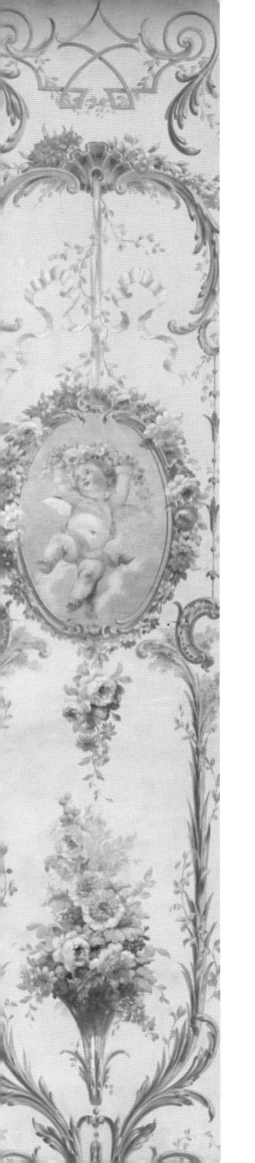

'Great results come from great contrasts.'

commissioned to transform it into a modern, clean space, using strong materials - wood, marble, steel and black glass panelled doors. The furniture in this apartment has an international feeling, mixed with a few well-chosen 18th century antiques and an important collection of Brazilian painting. So the old and the new came together well in the same space

Using colour is a challenge to many designers, but not to me. I grew up with colours and I love to mix them

'Luxury is going through a revival. People like luxury rather than a cold, minimal space.'

hunt hamilton zuch

Designer: Lynne Hunt. **Company:** Hunt Hamilton Zuch, London, UK.
Projects: Predominantly hotels and leisure work, plus residential projects, in
the UK and Europe. **Home:** A period house in London and a country home in
Sussex. **Hero:** Emile-Jacques Ruhlmann. **Inspiration:** Art Deco. **Love:** Timber
and natural textures. **Loathe:** Chintz.

● My style is both contemporary and classic, nothing too avant garde, and
quite simple. But I do like the odd twist, something that looks fun. It might be
a piece of artwork that helps pull everything together, or just an accent chair.

• The 1930s is a big influence. It's really a glamorous period and has a definite sense of modernity to it, fitting in very well with a contemporary environment • The '30s influence also comes through in some of the metals that I use, especially chrome, but also in something like the shape of a chair or in other materials, like leather • I have just done a penthouse where I used sycamore panelling in the living room, which worked out really well and created a light, almost iridescent feel. There was some ebony inlay as well, so it did have quite a Deco feeling • The penthouse was in an old hospital converted into contemporary apartments. We put in some columns to divide up the space, which were wrapped with aluminium and we also used a lot of mirrors to help reflect the views • We certainly played with colours a little bit in that project - a little black for punch and glamour, pistachio green for one of the guest bedrooms and a lilac purple for the master bedroom • There are real connections between our hotel

work and residential projects. A lot of apartment blocks now have communal areas with a lot of the things you would expect to find in a hotel - swimming pools, health suites, gyms, treatment rooms ● People's expectations are much higher and they are upgrading their own homes to hotel standards in terms of things like power showers, bathrooms or sound systems ● The cross-over works the other way as well, with many of our hotel clients looking for a residential feeling, a feeling of home and of individuality. But then people also expect something special and a little more glamorous in a hotel.

Designer: Zeynep Fadillioglu. **Company:** Zeynep Fadillioglu Interior Design, Istanbul, Turkey. **Projects:** Private houses, restaurants, offices and gardens in Turkey and elsewhere. **Home:** A house in Istanbul and an apartment in London. **Heroes:** Ed Tuttle, Tom Dixon, Anouska Hempel, Frank Gehry. **Inspiration:** Travel, film and fashion designers such as Yohji Yamamoto. **Love:** Antique pieces, such as Ottoman textiles, mixed in a contemporary environment. **Loathe:** Pastiches of set historical periods. Being tied to one period look is too restrictive.

• My inspiration mainly comes from my own background. I was born on the Bosporus, which separates two worlds. One side is Eastern, the other Western. Here the idea of East meets West is something very natural to us • I was brought up in a Venetian Ottoman house, full of textiles. That is

'I like to believe that, although our look is up to date, the work has more of a timeless quality to it.'

'There's such a mixture of cultures in Turkey and that carries into the design.'

reflected in my designs and I tend to use a lot of textiles and rich colours. But on the other hand I travel in the Far East, Africa, Italy and that is also reflected in our interiors ● I often bring antique pieces into a contemporary design. It might be just a detail, adding an Ottoman textile or cushion on a sofa, perhaps just a trimming, which brings in a sense of the unique ● I like to bring in different textures to create a sense of drama. I like making a feature of walls with finishes that catch the eye and introduce a little bit of theatre ● Even if we do a white wall, it won't just be a single white but a mix of many different shades. We did one project with a wall with small pieces of stone, like a hammam, so we tend to go for a natural rather than an artificial look ● We're thinking a lot at the moment about changing lifestyles and how that affects the home. For instance, I don't like the idea of a fixed dining room. Why not eat in a bedroom, or a library, or outside, depending on the situation and who you are with? ● I prefer low level seating and using floor cushions. It makes a room more informal and cosy and helps bring people together. More and more these

days people are lounging - lying or sitting on a sofa or cushions. People want to relax ● With the ever increasing pace of our lives, outdoor spaces are also becoming more important. We have to create an atmosphere, somewhere for thought and peace and to be nearer to nature ● The relationship between inside and outside is very important. In Turkey we have been designing many gazebos and tents, for example, with dining and seating areas, sometimes with leather curtains and heaters to extend the season.

'I love colour and texture - I could never be a minimalist.'

Designers: Angie Diggle, Dima Velikovsky, Larisa Ramanova. Company: Artistic Design, Moscow, Russia. Projects: Residential projects in Moscow and Russia. Home: Homes in Moscow. Heroes: Dmitry Chechulin and Alexander Vlasov, Soviet architects of the 1940s and '50s. Inspiration: Fusing multi-cultural influences from around the world. Love: Distressed and aged wood, from driftwood to antique furniture. Loathe: Overdressed rooms and bad lighting.

• Our style is definitely international. Our clients are a sophisticated group of people who travel extensively, often have homes abroad as well as in Russia, and know what's out there. They know what's good and what they like • There's been a big move away here from ethnic Russian style, although a fantasy is to work on a traditional Russian dacha and restore and renovate it • We like the mix of antique and contemporary. For instance, we love heavy silk curtains but not with pattern, because that would be just too traditional. On the other hand we don't like modern dressings for

windows because they are too cold ● It's very difficult to live in a completely contemporary space. There has to be a comfort level and you only achieve that with some traditional elements which make you feel cosy and good about life. ● The 19th century Empire period is a favourite, with its heavy furniture. There are some amazing 19th century Russian antiques out there as well which also have a wonderful weight to them ● We make sure that from room to room there is a continuation of colour, perhaps just an echo. When you're mixing antique and contemporary pieces there has to be a reference between the pieces, otherwise they won't make sense together ● A client might walk into a house and won't quite know why a space works, or why it ties together. That's because the technique of tying old and new together is so subtle ● We hate themed rooms, where you might have an Oriental living room and then a traditional English period feeling for a bedroom. You have to choose a colour frame, or a set of materials, and create a mix around that.

● Cold Moscow winters can last seven months so you have to remind yourself of that when you are planning a space. It might be something as simple as where to put all those coats and shoes that you need outside when you come back home ● In the winter by three in the afternoon it's getting dark so we will play tricks with window treatments, such as hiding spotlights to brighten up window spaces. It's a trick to make you think there's still some sun outside.

'Russia has completely transformed itself in the last few years, which as a designer, is quite inspirational in itself.'

steve leung designers

Designer: Steve Leung. **Company:** Steve Leung Designers Ltd, Hong Kong. **Projects:** Mostly residential, including show apartments, plus restaurants, bars and offices in Hong Kong and China. **Home:** A ground floor garden apartment in Hong Kong. **Heroes:** Le Corbusier, Frank Gehry. **Inspiration:** Travel, especially in China, the surrounding environment. **Love:** Simple lines and furniture or architecture with a Chinese influence. **Loathe:** European classicism.

• There is definitely a strong Chinese influence to my work. Because I'm an architect as well as an interior designer, I studied Chinese architecture and visited many different parts of China. That has given me a lot of inspiration • I like the design of traditional Chinese quadrangle houses, especially in Beijing, which are built on a north/south axis and planned around a central courtyard garden. I have used similar ideas in my own work, but in a more contemporary way • I'm always looking at the design of antique Chinese furniture because I design my own furniture based on those traditional pieces. But my own designs are simple and modern in comparison • With my

'I like simple lines, a contemporary minimal style

but with elements of traditional Chinese design.'

'A modern minimalist style can tie in with a sense of richness or glamour, and with different cultural influences.'

furniture I use different types of timber: teak, rosewood and cherry. They are widely used in Chinese furniture and fit in with traditional craftsmanship. Low-tech methods are used to make a high fashion prcduct ● The Ming dynasty is my favourite era because it was such a civilised period and close to modern history and design. Some traditional pieces can have quite a contemporary feeling ● I always start with spatial planning before I try to dress something up. In Hong Kong space is very precious so we are trained to design in a very efficient manner. A garden or a courtyard, for instance, is quite a luxury in Hong Kong ● Folding doors or sliding partitions are another thing that you

find in a typical Chinese house that we like to use. That means spaces become flexible and can easily be divided up or opened out ● For bathrooms, we sometimes use wash basins designed like a water bowl, sitting on a counter. They are similar to bowls you find in old Chinese houses. Also, loose furniture like tables and counters in the bathroom have a traditional heritage ● Minimalism can be interpreted in a range of styles. It doesn't have to be cold or barren. It can also be very rich in terms of colours and materials, but with a simplicity in the detailing of the space.

etchika werner einrichtungen

Designer: Etchika Werner. **Company:** Etchika Werner Einrichtungen, Berlin, Germany. **Projects:** Private houses and apartments, hotels, offices and other public projects. **Home:** An apartment in a 19th century building in Berlin. Shortly moving to Potsdam. **Heroes:** Karl Friedrich Schinkel, Anouska Hempel. **Inspiration:** Photography and photographs, as well as the environment. **Love:** Beautiful fabrics and natural materials. **Loathe:** Plastic.

• We are doing a lot of work in Berlin at the moment - a hotel, some private apartments and houses, and working with all kinds of buildings. It's a very exciting time in the city. Every day the city is changing and becoming more international • We often work with traditional buildings and many of our clients have a love of 18th or 19th century design. But at the same time we have also been creating some more contemporary, understated interiors, so we have to be versatile • We prefer to work with a 19th century building where there is more space, high ceilings, good windows. The period features inside are often very beautiful as well, because the architects designed with an eye on outside and in • Today many architects design buildings with an emphasis only on the exterior. They don't bother to think about inside. But the two have to go together so as to be in harmony • We often spend a lot of time restoring what we can in a

'For me, beauty is the most important consideration.'

period building. Many of these houses are protected so we have to be careful about what we do. We will use traditional materials, designs and colours • But with the furniture we will mix the old and the new, sometimes bringing in pieces that are very modern. Creating that mix and getting it right is instinctive. There is no set formula • We do bring in influences from France and England, which is very important. In Germany we don't have the same variety of design and designers and it often seems that what is happening in France or England in design, is more vibrant • Our design tradition was

'We adapt our style to the building and to the client. We like to do something different every time.'

broken for a long time and it's taken many years for a new generation of designers to establish themselves. It will take perhaps 100 years to really revive Germany's design tradition ● In France we tend to look for classical and period designs - 18th and 19th century style. But in England we also look at more contemporary design ● Personally I like to have bright colours, both beautiful and rich. But I often have to persuade the client because there is a great deal of conservatism. They often prefer to have calmer, more neutral colours ● I like to use aubergine, celadon, Chinese lacquer-style reds. I used to hate orange, but now I love orange. So the influences on you do change and the way that you see things evolves all the time.

joseph sy & associate

Designer: Joseph Sy. **Company:** Joseph Sy & Associate, Hong Kong. **Projects:** Residential projects, commercial, restaurants and hotels in Hong Kong and mainland China, including Beijing and Shanghai. **Home:** A contemporary apartment in Hong Kong. **Heroes:** Tadoa Ando, Frank Gehry and Philippe Starck. **Inspiration:** Travel, architecture and music. **Love:** Strong colours and good lighting. **Loathe:** Cluttered spaces.

• I tend to look at interiors from a broader perspective, rather than looking very closely at finishing and detailing, however important they may be. It's the overall picture

that's most important to me ● My style is straight forward, contemporary, unpretentious and very uncluttered ● I have an awareness of classical principles of scale and symmetry ● I always like to look forward rather than back to what has gone before. I don't have a passion about a particular period in design that I'm trying to reproduce. The future is much more interesting than the past ● My approach to interiors is very architectural. I worked as an architect for a long time before moving into interiors, so I think we see things in a different way. We have the advantage of a better understanding of space and structural possibilities ● I am very interested in Japanese architecture and architects, such as Tadoa Ando. I like the serenity of modern Japanese spaces and the radicalism of their architects. They have a real willingness to experiment ● For restaurants and public spaces designers can be much bolder with colour than they would be in the home. These are places for entertainment and life, so there's more opportunity to experiment with primary colours - reds, blues and greens ● In Hong Kong especially,

'To me a simple plan is the best plan.'

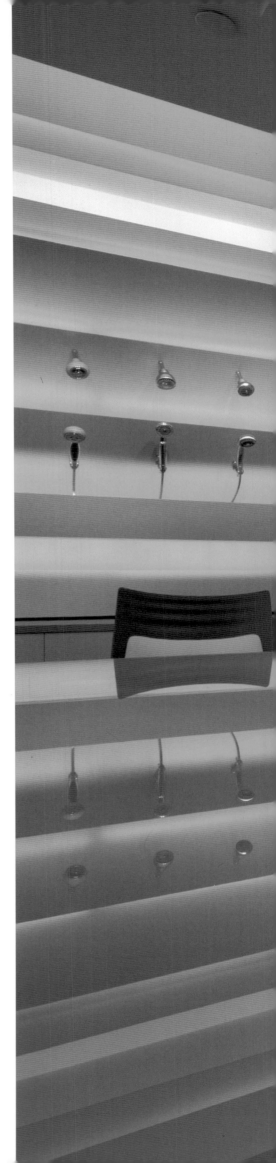

space is at a premium. It means you have to be more inventive with the home, creating - for instance - hidden beds in a living space that can be revealed and folded down to make a sleeping area ● It's a challenge to create multi-functional spaces and to make the most of the space that's available. We'll use sliding doors and screens to create flexible spaces, such as a kitchen, which can be either open plan or sectioned off.

'I think we see things in a different way, a more architectural way, compared to many interior designers.'

gernot uhlenburg einrichtungshaus

Designers: Marja Schwartz, Gernot Uhlenburg. **Company:** Gernot Uhlenburg Einrichtungshaus, Rottach-Egern, Bavaria, Germany. **Projects:** Private homes in Germany, Austria and Mallorca. **Home:** A house in Bavaria. **Heroes:** None. **Inspiration:** Travelling, especially Asia. **Love:** Natural colours, natural materials. **Loathe:** Aggressive colours and fabrics.

● We don't like it when you go into a house and instantly recognise who the interior designer is. A house should reflect its owner, not the designer ● It's important to spend a lot of time right at the beginning of a project thinking about your client's way of living. You have to become a psychologist and find a way of interpreting their own ideas and bringing them to life ● Our work mixes traditional elements or antiques with modern, contemporary ideas. But our designs always have to fit in with the region where we're working so it's important for us that the interior is in sympathy with the building itself ● The setting of a house is very important. We do a lot of work in Mallorca as well as Germany, and what we do in Mallorca has to be very different ● In Mallorca

'You need to think carefully about creating interiors that won't date in a year. Anything too fashionable, too of the minute, has a short shelf-life.'

we take account of the surroundings and use local materials where we can, as well as traditional paint techniques. We also try to use warmer colours - reds and bright Mediterranean colours ● In Bavaria its good to use pieces from Asia, because traditional Bavarian country style has a synergy with furniture designs from Asia, in both the materials and design ● We love Asian antiques. Gernot has been travelling to Asia and collecting furniture for the past twenty years. The things we like to use have to have a special texture, things you like to touch as well as look at.

'An interior designer shouldn't just impose his or her own style and way of thinking on a client's house. That's self-importance.'

contents & directory of designers

4
Amanda Rosa Interiors
The Space
26 Holland Street
Glasgow G2 4LR
0141 227 6262

16
Antoni Associates
5th Floor, 186 Loop Street
Cape Town 8001
South Africa
0027 21 422 2406

22
Heiberg Cummings Design Ltd
548 West 28th Street # 510
NY 10001
New York
001 212 239 4470

30
Clifton Property
Developments Ltd
Hebe House
38 William V Street
London WC2N 4DD
020 7351 6912

34
Serdar Gülgün
Husrev Gerede
Caddesi Gozum
Apt. no. 69 D.3
80200 Tesvikiye
Istanbul
0090 212 261 1840

40
Richard Daniels Design
The Old School Hall
10 Wiseton Road
London SW17 7EE
020 8767 8428

50
Trendson Interieur
Schoutetstraat 4
2800 Mechelen
Belgium
0032 15 21 02 60

56
Lifestyles (Interiors) Ltd
48 Old Church Street
London SW3 5BY
020 7349 8020

64
Pia Maria Schmid Architektur
& Designburo
Augustinergasse 25
8001 Zurich
Switzerland
0041 1 221 08 48

68
Anna Bilton
6 Passmore Street
London SW1W 8HP
020 7730 4267

76
Kit Kemp
Firmdale Hotels
18 Thurloe Place
London SW7 2SP
020 7581 4045

86
Joanna Trading Ltd
7 Bunhouse Place
London SW1W 8HU
020 7730 0693

94
Yoo Too
2 Bentinck Street
London W1U 2FA
020 7009 0100

100
Hennie Interiors
Bennechesgt 1
0169 Oslo
Norway
0047 22 06 85 86

106
Carter Tyberghein
Hyde Park House
Manfred Road
London SW15 2RS
020 8871 4800

112
B.V.B.A. Giardini
Kapellensteenweg 544
2920 Heide-Kalmthout
Belgium
0032 36 66 74 17

118
Estudio f. Interiores
C/Maestro Perez Cabrero
08001 Barcelona
Spain
0034 932 41 10 38

122
Louise Bradley
15 Walton Street
London SW3 2HX
020 7589 1442

132
Olivier Antoine Decorateur
Villa le Colombier
238 Route du Chateau
06340 Drap
France
0033 49 32 73 662

138
Société Christine Gérondeau
Decoration
69 Boulevard Barbes
75018 Barbes
Paris
00331 42 23 54 07

142
Candy & Candy
5 Lower Belgrave Street
London SW1W ONR
020 7824 7520

150
Head Interiors
P.O. BOX 87138
Houghton 2041
South Africa
00 27 11 325 27 00
&
3 Prince Albert Road
London NW1 7SN
020 7482 0379

156
Homeira Pour Heidari
Lucile Grahn Strasse 38
81675 Munich
Germany
0049 172 672 7647

166
Francois Champsaur
56 rue du Faubourg St Antoine
Cour du Bel Air
75012 Paris
00331 434 52246

170
Hecker Phelan
Unit 3c, Oxford Street
Collingwood
3066 Victoria
Australia
00 613 9417 0466

176
Taylor Howes
208 The Chambers
Chelsea Harbour
London SW10 OXF
020 7349 9017

186
Joao Mansur Arquitetura
& Design
Rua Groenlandia 1922B
01434-100 Jd. America
Sao Paulo
Brazil
0055 11 30 83 15 00

194
Hunt Hamilton Zuch
Studio G2
Chelsea Reach
79-89 Lots Road
London SW10 ORN
020 7795 1113

200
Zeynep Fadillioglu
A. Adnan Saygun cad.
Canan Sokak
Rifat Bey apt. no 4/2
80630 Ulus
Istanbul
Turkey
0090212 287 0936

208
Artistic Design
Moscow, 103001
U1 Spiridonovka
9/2 kv. 070
Russia
007 095 203 3397

212
Steve Leung Designers Ltd
2401-02, CC Wu Building
302 Hennessy Road
Wanchai
Hong Kong
0085 22 52 71 600

218
Etchika Werner
Fasanenstrasse 68
10719 Berlin
Germany
0049 30 881 46 00

226
Joseph Sy & Associate Ltd
17/F Heng Shan Centre
145 Queen's Road East
Wanchai
Hong Kong
0085 22 86 61 333

232
Gernot Uhlenburg
Einrichtungshaus GmbH
Ludwig-Thoma-Strasse 7
D-83700 Rottach-Egern
AM Tegernsee
Germany
0049 8022 26014